POPCORN COUNTRY

The Story of America's Favorite Snack

Cris Peterson

Photographs by
David R. Lundquist

BOYDS MILLS PRESS
AN IMPRINT OF HIGHLIGHTS
Honesdale, Pennsylvania

To Violet & Cora
—CP

To my significant other, Randee, and our combined and precious eight grandchildren—Keenan, Isaac, Lucas, Christopher, Sloane, Harper, Reagan, and Bernadette
—DRL

How do you like your popcorn?

Bathed in melted butter? Kettle cooked with sugar and salt? Slathered in gooey caramel? Or gobbled by the bucket at the movie theater?

Any way you munch it, popcorn is one of America's favorite treats. Every year we devour four and a half billion gallons of the stuff. That's enough to fill the Empire State Building from top to bottom eighteen times!

But America's love of popcorn isn't half as amazing as how it is grown and turned into the best snack there is.

Popcorn comes from the land of wind turbines and flat-as-a-pancake prairie. This part of our country is called the Corn Belt, a swath of fertile land that reaches from Ohio to Nebraska. Over ninety million acres of corn are grown each year in the United States but only a tiny portion of that is popcorn.

There are four kinds of corn grown in the United States:
dent corn, also called field corn, sweet corn, flint corn, and popcorn.

Most of the corn you see while traveling through the Midwest is *dent corn*, and it is grown mainly to feed livestock such as cattle, hogs, and chickens. Its ears are usually larger than other kinds of corn, and its kernels become indented when the corn is dried. That's why it's called dent corn. You can't pop dent corn.

Sweet corn is the type that we eat right off the cob. It contains more sugar than any other corn. The sweet corn plant is usually a bit shorter than dent corn, and the ears are picked when the kernels are tender and juicy. You can't pop sweet corn either.

Flint corn, which is sometimes called Indian corn, is named for its hard kernels and comes in a multitude of colors. It is a close relative of popcorn, but it doesn't pop very well.

Popcorn has the smallest ear of all. When the corn is ready to harvest, the kernels are shiny, golden, and hard as rocks. You can't eat popcorn unless it is popped.

Popcorn seeds are planted in April or early May. The long, straight rows of popcorn will be knee-high by the Fourth of July. By August, the field will be a jungle of rigid green stalks, rustling leaves, and skittering bugs. Roots reaching over six feet into the ground pull moisture and nutrients into plants that stretch so tall that they could tickle the chin of a young giraffe (that's about ten feet tall). It takes twenty-five inches of rainfall to grow a crop of popcorn. By fall, the popcorn is ready to pop.

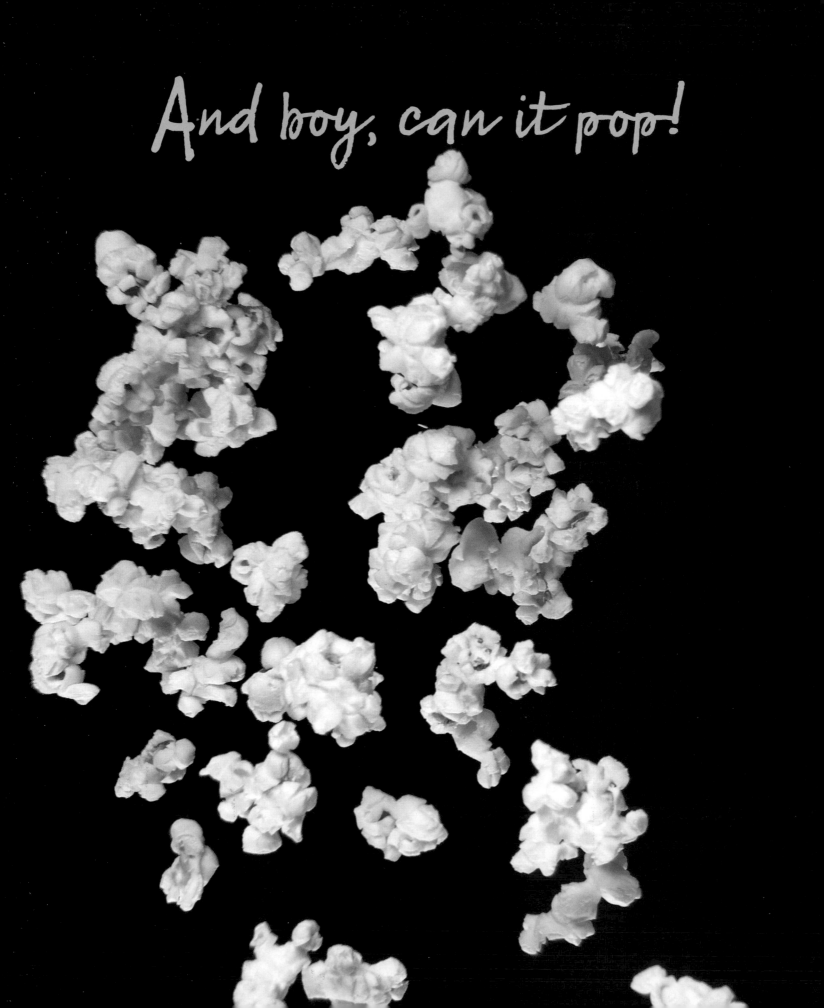

And boy, can it pop!

If all twenty million kernels of popcorn on one acre of land (about the size of a football field) popped at once, piles of the white, fluffy snack would cover the ground like four inches of snow.

But popcorn can't pop right out of the field. It first has to be harvested. Giant mechanical harvesters called combines roll across the prairie and separate the ears of corn from the plant.

The dry leaves that cover the ears are called husks. The husks and pieces of cob are discharged from the back of the combine as the golden kernels are shelled from the cobs.

The kernels pour into the grain tank at the top of the combine. Then trucks haul the popcorn to a processing facility where one hundred sixty million kernels per truckload are unloaded into big silver bins. The popcorn is "conditioned," or dried, in the bins to just the right amount of moisture for popping.

Next, the popcorn travels on a conveyor to the processing room where the grain dances across jiggling screens that shake broken kernels and pieces of corn cob out of the popcorn. Then it travels to a vibrating gravity table. Big blowy fans cause the grain to tumble in the air.

The lighter popcorn kernels and any remaining bits of husk and cob fall away and only the "just right" kernels stay on the machine. The kernels fly by an electronic eye that checks for uniform color. If a kernel is discolored, a blast of air shoots it off the processor.

Finally, the popcorn is ready to test for pop-ability. A half pound of every truckload of popcorn is tested in a specially designed kettle-style popper that looks like the poppers you see in movie theaters. The testing lab smells like a movie theater lobby.

As the waterproof hull, or outside of the kernel, heats up in hot oil, the bit of moisture inside it turns to steam, and the steam softens the starch in its center. The pressure inside the kernel builds and builds until the temperature reaches 347 degrees and the starch turns to liquid.

Then *BOOM!* It explodes.

The tiny steam-powered bomb pops inside out. In a fraction of a second it cools and solidifies into a crunchy treat. The popped corn is then poured into a large tube to measure its volume. If the moisture in each kernel isn't just right, the popcorn won't pop big enough to meet the standard set by the processor. When it passes the pop-ability test, it is ready for the final packing step.

WATTS 60 Hz
S-488-8465

NSF.

MFG.
09-Sep-14

WARNING! CONTACT WITH THIS
SURFACE WHILE THE APPLIANCE
IS OPERATING MAY CAUSE BURNS

AVERTISSEMENT! CONTACT AVEC
CETTE SURFACE PENDANT LE
FONCTIONNEMENT DE L'APPAREIL
POURRAIT CAUSER DES BRULURES
67087

The popcorn kernels are ready to bag and ship out. Some popcorn is packaged in microwave bags. Some is poured into jars or bags for movie theaters, sports venues, and grocery stores. And much of the popcorn is loaded into one-ton tote bags that look like giant white building blocks.

The totes travel by truck to the Great Lakes where they are loaded onto container ships and sailed across the Atlantic Ocean to countries all over the world. Some totes travel on barges down the Mississippi River to the Gulf of Mexico where more container ships are waiting. The United States produces nearly all of the world's popcorn.

The magical sound of popcorn popping and the irresistible aroma of a heaping bowl of fluffy, flaky goodness is a treat nearly everyone enjoys. One of the most loved snacks in the world explodes into buttery deliciousness and makes parties, movies, and carnivals extra special.

America is popcorn country, and popcorn is America's gift to the world.

A History of Popcorn

Popcorn is one of America's oldest snacks. Archaeologists found four-thousand-year-old kernels at a site called Bat Cave in New Mexico—and some could still pop. Aztec Indians in Mexico used popcorn as a decoration and a food over two thousand years ago. And French explorers who paddled their canoes through the Great Lakes region four hundred years ago met Iroquois Indians making popcorn by burying it in hot sand until it popped. That must have been a gritty treat!

Popcorn didn't come to modern American kitchens until whalers and sailors brought it home to New England all the way from South America in the 1820s. And it really didn't catch on as a snack until 1893 when a huge world's fair in Chicago called the Columbian Exposition was held. Over twenty-seven million people attended the fair during the six months it was open. They rode on the first Ferris wheel, tasted Shredded Wheat and Juicy Fruit gum for the first time, and ate A LOT of popcorn.

Inventor and candy store owner, Charles Cretors, brought his new-fangled steam-powered popcorn machine to the fair. No one paid too much attention to his exhibit the first couple days, so Cretors decided to give his popcorn away. "Free popcorn!" he shouted. The mouth-watering smell of hot, buttery popcorn combined with the magical sound of corn popping drifted down the Midway, and fairgoers flocked to Cretors' cart.

His steam engine with a red-suited toy clown on top frantically cranking the popper was nearly as much of an attraction as the free popcorn. After a few days Cretors began to charge for his treat, but the long lines at his cart never dwindled.

By the 1920s popcorn was everywhere . . . at baseball games, circuses, carnivals, and parks. It finally made its way to the movies when talking pictures were introduced in 1927. Along with the delicious bags of fresh popcorn came Cracker Jack, a boxed mixture of popcorn, peanuts, and molasses that was first introduced at the 1893 Chicago Columbian Exposition. Today, over a hundred years after its introduction, two hundred million boxes of Cracker Jack sell each year in America.

Sources

BOOKS

American Popcorn Company. *Jolly Time: An American Tradition Since 1914*. Sioux City, IA: American Pop Corn Company, 1994.

DePaola, Tomie. *The Popcorn Book*. New York, NY: Holiday House, 1978.

Giedt, Frances Towner. *Popcorn!* New York, NY: Simon & Schuster, 2004.

Myers, Jack. *What Makes Popcorn Pop?: And Other Questions About the World Around Us*. Honesdale, PA: Boyds Mills Press, 1994.

Smith, Andrew F. *Popped Culture: A Social History of Popcorn in America*. Washington, DC: Smithsonian Institution, 2001.

Topping, Robert W. *Just Call Me Orville: The Story of Orville Redenbacher*. West Lafayette, IN: Purdue University Press, 2011.

Woodside, David. *What Makes Popcorn Pop?* New York, NY: Atheneum, 1980.

WEBSITES*

Cretors.com
cretors.com/page.asp?i=12

Charles Cretors invented the modern popcorn popper and introduced it at the 1893 Columbian Exposition in Chicago. Cretors popcorn poppers are still made today.

Popcorn.org

Funded by the non-profit popcorn growers association, the website features the history, science, and little-known facts about popcorn.

Scientificamerican.com
scientificamerican.com/article/explore-the-pop-in-popcorn

This website explores the "pop" in popcorn through a very clearly written science project. Key concepts in physics, gases, plant science, and food science are explored.

Smithsonian.com
smithsonianmag.com/arts-culture/why-do-we-eat-popcorn-at-the-movies-475063

The history of how popcorn became a movie theater staple.

TheScienceexplorer.com
thescienceexplorer.com/nature/what-makes-popcorn-pop

Includes a slow-motion video of corn popping and the scientific explanation of the process.

The Science and History of Popcorn
youtube.com/watch?v=qA1XfVDXoMc

An entertaining, fact-filled twelve-minute YouTube video on the history and science of popcorn and how it saved the movie industry.

*Websites active at time of publication.

The author thanks Dan Sleaford, Field Production at Weaver Popcorn Country Inc. and member of the USDA Popcorn Board, Forest City, Illinois, for his careful review of the text and photography.

Boyds Mills Press
An Imprint of Highlights
815 Church Street
Honesdale, Pennsylvania 18431
boydsmillspress.com
Printed in China

ISBN: 978-1-62979-892-9
Library of Congress Control Number: 2018945686

First edition
10 9 8 7 6 5 4 3 2 1

The text is set in Bodoni Egyptian Pro.